the needle can

An Anthology of Poetry

Edited by

TERESA MEI CHUC

the needle can

ISBN: 978-0-9907958-0-3

Front cover: Sculpture art, Untitled, Wood and Tar, 1990, by Paul Bowen
Back cover art: Bleed, 2007, monotype, by Paul Bowen
Inside art: Dragger, 2005, monotype and walnut ink, by Paul Bowen

Published by Shabda Press
Pasadena, CA 91107
www.shabdapress.com

"The Sailor cannot see the North,
but knows the Needle can."

- Emily Dickinson

Contents

CX DILLHUNT

The Mirror Poem

Mirror: a reflective surface, now typically of glass coated with a metal amalgam, that reflects a clear image.

—New Oxford American Dictionary

The symbolism of mirrors depends not only on what things cause the reflection— nature, a book, drama—but also on what one sees in them—oneself, the truth, the ideal, illusion.

—A Dictionary of Literary Symbols

To begin with, there is no mirror on the wall. No one-way mirror. No two-way mirror. No rear-view mirror. No perfect mirror. This is not a poem about reflectivity. Nor the Venus effect as far as I can see. This is not a poem about water, about Narcissus. There are no flowers in this poem. This poem occasionally suffers from bouts of spectrophobia, worries about its substrate, and longs for a more clear understanding of its silvering process. If this poem is made of glass it is unaware.

If this poem thinks of itself as anything, it can quickly become catoptrophobic and from time to time has been known to lean toward its eisoptrophobic tendencies. For protection this poem wears mirror armor rondels to ward off the eyes of evil.

On Tuesdays in May, this poem has been found wandering the prairie in search of meaning, but is content to be discontent. Once it was found hanging out on a bridge pretending to understand the proper construction of the infinity mirror. When this poem is at its best it makes long lists of things others find reflected in its deep sheen of meaning. Yesterday, it found the meaning of light, or so it thought. Later, it realized it was on the wrong page and that although it was part of a book it had lost its ability to cause its own reflection.

This evening, if there's enough time, this poem might search out new methods of mirror writing, read a few books citing references as old as 6200 BCE, and continue its investigation into reflective, refractive, and other transparent materials and objects including kaleidoscopes and lasers for precise poetics.

BATCH

1. *My mother's recipe,* my mother always said.
Make a big batch, I always said.

ORIGIN: Current senses date from early
childhood through mid-teens.

In the winter, I lived for the open oven door,
the glory of the blue flames dancing tipped in yellow,
*the entire **batch** she made this morning long gone.*

2. Bake. Make. More here than meets the eye.

3. Formula. Purposeful. More at: *I've heard of*
adding cryolite, cutting back the borax, and leaving
out the arsenic.

4. Remembrance, a recipe: *Soda, lime. I'm made.*
As in: *I'm my mother's **batch**. I've read how*
re-baking doesn't help, weakens brotherhood.

See: **GREENLAND, OTHERLAND,**
BROTHERLAND

Also: **BLISTER,** *esp. def., 2*

BLISTER

1. Imperfection. As if to say: *You, you are an artist,*
you are no bubble. You are not a pimple, your
swelling does not disgust me.

2. Bubble. As in: *You are not the ruin of my work,*
you are the direction I take, you are my brother.

3. A remembrance; which is to say: *Brother,*
an other, a blister on time, our friction, our bubbles filled
with the irritants of our lives.

To remember; more at: *A memory, our memory. Remember? We are glass, we are blistered.*

To know no one wants us, but we want each other. As in: *Blood brothers. Blister brothers.*

4. Perfection.

5. A certain calmness, doneness, oneness. You sitting there in your chair, listening, glistening, no chair needed, the air knows how to hold you now. In control. Flat-out-unflat.

See: **BATCH, BUBBLE** *Also:* **SEED**

Perhaps (compare): **BLISTER BEETLE**
Also (related): **REFLEXIVE BLEEDING**

BUBBLE

1. Unknown knowingness; no need to polish.

2. Begunness. A certain certainness, full, filledness. As if to say: *Blessed wretchedness hung on to too long, ready to pop together (more at: **pimple**).*

3. Beyond together. Bread-like. A-baking. Brethren.

In this sense, synonymous with **BLISTER.**
As in: *bubble other, bubble brother, bubble mother.*

from <u>The Incomplete Glass Man's Glossary</u>

A Glass Haibun for Line & Longing

Line / to count on / wait
on / end of the / begin / lin-
eage / leaded / long

Longing is longer than is imaginable. Longing is the middle of the Middle Ages. Longing is the middle of the middle of the night. Longing is not the waking but what wakes you. Longing is the groove in the H-shaped cross section of the longest line of lead that you can ever remember that was prepared by the glazier for a stained glass window you have never seen. Longing is the length of the longest line of lead in the rose window in the north transept of St. Joseph's Basilica on the bank of the Fox River in West De Pere, Wisconsin on the day you were baptized by Abbot Bernard Pennings, who you were told also baptized your mother over the same baptismal font. Longing is what calls you by name and says that longing has no name. Longing is how we all lie. Longing is longer than dying. Longing is the length of longing is what longing was and longer.

The Litany of St. Mark the Evangelist: Patron Saint of Glaziers and Stained Glass Workers

Et infideles universos ad Evangelii lumen perducere digneris, *Te rogamus, audi nos.*

[Lord, please lead all unbelievers to the light of the Gospel, *We beseech You, hear us.*]

—***Litaniae Sanctorum, c. 785***
Abbaye Saint-Pierre de Solesmes

St. Glass, *Pray for us.*
Sts. Glazed In & Glazed Over, *Pray for us.*
St. Glazier, *Pray for us.*

St. Stained Glass, *Pray for us.*
Sts. Glassy, Glassier & Glassiest, *Pray for us.*
St. Paté de Verre, *Pray for us.*

St. Settings of Contrasting Colors, *Pray for us.*
St. Form of Decorative Designs, *Pray for us.*
Sts. Colorful Glass & Leaded Framework, *Pray for us.*

Sts. Transparent & Translucent, *Pray for us.*
St. Edges of Refraction, *Pray for us.*
Sts. Vitreous & Companions, *Pray for us.*

St. Homogeneous Material, *Pray for us.*
St. Random with Liquid-like & Non-crystalline
    Molecular Structures, *Pray for us.*
Sts. Annealing & Annealed, *Pray for us*

Sts. Fused by Firing & Finished, *Pray for us.*
Sts. Scatter, Shatter & Shard, *Pray for us.*
Sts. Knop, Nappy & Nef, *Pray for us.*

St. Lens & All Optical Instruments Containing
 a Lens or Lenses, *Pray for us*
Sts. Monoculus & Ocula, *Pray for us*
St. Telescopius & All the Magnifiers of Our
 Heavens, *Pray for us*

All You Holy Windows with Your Entering &
 Entertaining Light, *Intercede for us.*

All You Holy Makers, Takers & Breakers of
 Light, *Intercede for us.*

All You Colors, You Tones, You Shades &
 Your Endless Shadows, *Intercede for us.*

O, Father of Glass & Glassmakers, Make us Glass,
Color our lives with the Light of Your Stained Windows
proving again the Virgin Birth, the Flatness of Earth.

O, Evangelist, Fill our Vessels with the Words of Your
Color & Light, Rain upon us with All the Glories of
these Unshatterable Syllables of our Unbreakable Faith.

O, Patron of Glaziers & Stained Glass Workers, of Venice,
of Opticians, & of All Things Glass, Stain us with All the
Light & All the Color of Your Cathedrals, Again & Again.

LENS

a
noun
a piece
of glass cur-
ved concentrating
light dispersing rays used singly
as in this poem or a group of light gathering de-
vices such as a gloss or a glossary not to be confused with glass eyes or tongues

DERIVATIVES: **unlensed, lenslessness**; OR, though less uncommon, but nonetheless a sometimes useful variation: **lensful,** as in: *She was so bright this morning as to appear **lensful**.*

See: **lensing, unlensing;** *Sometimes:* **relensing.**

USAGE NOTE ON ***RELENSING*:** Often mindful of its origin and referring to its grain-like substance or happenstance; usually poetic, but sometimes spiteful or ungracious; as in: *The argument about the **relensing** of his poem led to much discussion, none of which revealed any insight into the shape of his meaning.*

from The Incomplete Glass Man's Glossary

DREW DILLHUNT

The concept of remedy is tenuous at best

when your mother sits with you
in the kitchen chair, your arms around her neck. There,
I reach over her shoulder, coax down your lower lid—
run a bead of erythromycin along the redness.
Excess is caught up in your lashes
as you work your swollen eyes—
a scrim of clear gel that blurs everything:

the tenuousness of conception is a remedy at last.

Eye-let

after Katalin Szlukovenyi's poem "Ihlet"

Mint kudzu sink on tarmac's fuel lock—
a Hunger System. Mirror-fog bezel nigh
as vocal maim sinks. (Hog emit fog.) Mundane, aye.
A vat reflects all airtime, forty-tome.
Daily core, nay. Come, same-bile logos, marry.
Can I, a rogue, a shone vague, improvise a look?
Keep out loam, a home, a lie (or she's a God).
Edgy mugful lay low, merit-panel all.
Eyes low, whole look stove-throb: a hung nye moon.
Magellan eyes I gauze, isle velvet
my core, a rotten-winged marquee sit
rest key, rise knees seltzer hall, a straw nonsenses
ford, dilute, join. O, canal amulets pare out.
Mazel tov, heli-lot—a show, serentity.
Ford a pass, adding catalog as a gambit
adding geo-dome key. You roam. Probable goes home.
Fennel gondola, toenail eyes saves seven.
Formula at make, at meek, rail leek.
Edgy vale or sign, utensil, gouge haystack
tune. O, key phage say rays, whole cheeky moon-dome
a core airtime merge mirror-short—a hand.

Leaf is All

A feather is a weighty construct
once fossilized
impervious to the clock radio

Of flowers, spread athwart the garden, Aye,

how to explain a pear is not a pearl—
memories as vigilant as trying

to back up the drive.
Standing on the wall, you're the height
of the city when we embrace

the real numbers disappear *Papa,*
I don't believe in _____. *What do you think?*

The traffic is distraught. We *are* traffic

practically, about the moment
on the count of three I put the ducklings in my pocket

Took now this form, now that, in swift succession!

Exemplars

We arrive on the Jumbotron like
the happenstance of a dugout

the way *umpire* sounds a touch
like *Empire.*

Entropy begins at the ocean of desire.
We have some friends, who have some friends

and tickets for the usher at the stairs.
From here, just east of home plate

I can see
all there is to love
about baseball.

This is life! I shout

to the little boy bobbing
in his father's arms

in time
to the music of the seventh-inning stretch.

We were propaganda for the moment,
the National Pastime of closing our eyes.

I'm hardly even chagrined
now
as I tell you

we reveled in it.

EMILY JOHNSTON

She looked away from her cup and out the window

She looked away from her cup and out the window
but it was dark—she likely saw   only herself
        and not me   on the sidewalk
walking a small dog.

        It was so long ago.
It seems that it hardly happened.

It's a disruptive
force, love, seldom fit for
polite company. Lovers have always
lied—for priests, spouses,
children, neighbors. What can you
do with it, in the end: the helplessness
the outrageous happiness?
We build lives of wood, and   love wants to burn.
So: I burned.
It happens all the time.

        It was so long ago.
It seems that it hardly happened.

So now, in a light spring rain, I'm half a block down
        and shivering. I was not a
figure of pathos when I left the house.   I was
a woman   enjoying an early May evening
walking a cherished friend.
I felt glad   even   animated
        by the rain: by solitude.
But her every movement was familiar once—
I feel them in my cells even still—and
the unfolding hours of her eyes—

never once, as tonight
       looking straight through me.

Why is it   the one   in darkness   who sees
       and why is that always me?

I was a coward, when she left. I did not break the glass.

She doesn't think that what she does matters

She doesn't think that what she does matters.
She loves her daughter very much.
The long commute
the flying   each summer
the private days at the edge
          of history
working, cooking, tinkering: not fighting
not furying
not stripping herself, habit by habit,
          bare of illusion—
clemency, continuity, tomorrow:
these days bear no relation—so small
her life—to the coming cataclysm. So
large the forces. So small her life.
She is tenacious to modest pleasures.
She is but
          one person.
She knows what's coming—
she fears it in her bones.
But the butterflies at her country acres—
who can resist
them, or the dusty pleasures
of picking cherries, building fences, walking the dog?
Yet she can't—she says—give up her job
          or find one closer   or live closer
     or   well, she *could*   but: therefore
the commute   & the lack of time
to devote—even to life
          on earth   which means of course her daughter.
She lives modestly. She's a kind
person, quick to help others. What's reasonable
                    to ask?
(I would like to be reasonable.)

Her wants—& those of nearly everyone else, 7 billion
        and counting counting counting
        counting counting—
do not seem excessive.
So like most people each morning she wakes
        she starts the engine again.
        in the mossy perfection
        of this jewelbox world
        she starts the engine
she hopes the hose is long enough
        that cataclysm takes awhile.

She loves her daughter very much.
She loves her daughter very much.

> "Those who dwell...among the beauties and mysteries of the earth
> are never alone or weary of life."
> —Rachel Carson

World is a blanket

World is a blanket.
In the night. In the snow. In the town.
The window glows yellow. The café's
hard envelope
black against blue night.
The panes dividing light
just so. Just feet
from the glass unruly the light
spreads again
growing and dimmer.
The snow is
everywhere.
Never alone or weary.

The cedar stands

The cedar stands
like a wraith
against the sea and sky.

You were there once
I think. I held you
and you were alive—
chilled and exhilarated at once.

Comfort is
no kind of life
you said, leaning
into me, but this—

The roots seem to float
atop the cliff.

Rain falls in sheets against me.

The cedar stands silent

The cedar stands silent
against the darkening
sea and sky—

a hundred feet away
    I read by a lamp:
families, wars, voyages.

No wind shakes the
panes nor scatters debris
in the dim-lit
streets inside me.

Like a wizard it beckons.
So much embedded in those cells—
how to thrive on rock and rain.

TERESA MEI CHUC

Gravity

I.
Tenderness that is
Transparent
Like this glass -
Vibrations, ringing.
The gravity of Trees
Pull us into their
Temples,
Pages of images swirl,
A flower emerges and
consumes us in its
triumphant beauty,
The weight of the
Encyclopedia of Flora
On your lap,
Persevering in our delight.
Next, some Chinese
numbers - yut, yee, sam...
Sounds of continents, consonants,
and vowels
Spin in constellations,
Laughter billows.

II.
We step into the floating darkness
To see your sunflowers,
Hidden behind a curtain of bushes,
Three stalks of exquisiteness
Pregnant with gold,
An interval in integral time,
Vertical,
In the center of the night.
Beyond, in the contours of shadows,
I almost stepped on the small purple
Flowers near the ground,
Exposed in its shining velvet – celestial.
In dim light, we looked
At radishes with anticipation
The fresh fragrance of mint leaves
Complement the night.

III.
Sipping time in abundance,
In spheres of inmost
Transformations,
Mingling with wind.
Above - a lighted window,
At this intersect of convergence,
A dawn in the tendril of darkness,
All that is intangible penetrates
Completely

Lemon

Soothing yellow acidic pleasure
Snaps off at the downward
Pull of a metal picker,
Abundant freshness
Topples
In a solitary thump!
I reach downwards
for the sun-colored conundrum,
placing it carefully on top
of the other lemons
cradled in my arms
that await to ultimately
become somebody's pie.

Grandma

Your hands glow of white jade,
Green flow of river veins,
Rice bowl in hands shaking,
Journey to the table,
On Chinese New Year red-dyed
watermelon seeds
cracked between false teeth leak
scent and red into hands,
Where decades ago my
tiny fingers reposed.

Campfire Conversation

at Pismo Beach

We watch the firewood burn
The flames
A marimba of fire
You stacked the pieces of wood
So that there is a chamber of embers
at the bottom
Orange hotter than our oven
And I try to fathom a heat that is over 800 degrees

You tell me that the burning wood
is releasing the sun's energy
How trees take in sunlight
and through photosynthesis
grow wood, leaves

How we are all made of sunlight
All the things we eat have eaten
what grows from the light of the sun

And I contemplate the vastness
of this special star that our planet
revolves around
and I feel a connection with
the universe as I had never felt before.

And I ask you about the container
for our campfire
What is it made of?
And you tell me iron
The same iron that my car is made of
The same iron that is in my blood

We look at the stars above us
whose light took thousands of years
to travel to us
whose light is a part of us

And you tell me about the earth's
elements that are inside of me
that I need to survive
Magnesium, zinc, copper,
manganese

You tell me that there is gold
inside of me, too.

Like the Dandelion Seeds

Like the dandelion seeds that
travel on the shoulders of a breeze,
your body not yet ready for
the mechanics of transportation.
I'm your only means of getting
from the living room to the kitchen.

Bios

CX Dillhunt was born in Green Bay and is fluent in the Wisconsin dialect. He learned to write and to tell stories from his mother, to sing and to pray from his father; he is grateful for his six brothers and five sisters for magnifying these gifts and teaching him confidence and how to play with others. CX is author of *Girl Saints* (Fireweed, 2003), *Things I've Never Told Anyone* (Parallel, 2007), and editor of *Hummingbird Magazine of the Short Poem* www.hummingbirdpoetry.org

Drew Dillhunt is author of the online chapbook *3,068,518* (*Mudlark,* No. 39, 2010). His writing has also appeared in *VOLT, Eclectica, Jacket2,* and *Tarpaulin Sky*. He was selected as a finalist for the 2009 National Poetry Series. His first full-length poetry collection, *Leaf is All,* is forthcoming from Bear Star Press in 2015. Drew is a member of the Seattle-based band Answering Machines, and the Associate Editor of *Hummingbird Press*.

Emily Johnston is a Seattle writer; her first book, *Her Animals,* is forthcoming from *Hummingbird Press* in 2015. She has also been published in *Slate, Rain Taxi, Truthout, The Oregonian,* and *The Stranger.*

Teresa Mei Chuc is the author of two poetry books, *Red Thread* (Fithian Press, 2012) and *Keeper of the Winds* (FootHills Publishing, 2014). Her poetry appears in numerous journals and anthologies and is forthcoming in the anthology, *Inheriting the War: Poetry and Prose by Descendants of Vietnam Veterans and Refugees.* Teresa's new poetry book, *Song of Bones,* is forthcoming from Many Voices Press in 2016.

Acknowledgments

"Gravity," "Lemon," "Grandma" and "Like the Dandelion Seeds" was first published online in the chapbook, *Cartography of Family* (Chippens Press)

The poem *Exemplars* first appeared in *TILL*

The italicized lines in "Leaf is All" are from Goethe's poem *The Metamorphosis of Plants* (except where they aren't)

www.ingramcontent.com/pod-product-compliance
Lightning Source LLC
Chambersburg PA
CBHW072055040426
42447CB00012BB/3137